THE GRAND PIANO RANGE

BOOKS BY SIBYL JAMES

THE GRAND PIANO RANGE

Sibyl James

Black Heron Press
Post Office Box 13396
Mill Creek, Washington 98082
www.blackheronprress.com

These poems in *The Grand Piano Range* have previously been published in the following publications: *The Arts*: "Her Big Scene," "Twisp, Washington," "Chinese Mines," Sacajawea Could Have Told Us," "The town tavern in Fairbury, Illinois," "Literacy," "Guazapa, El Salvador," "The Shrine to Saint Theresa"; *Ocooch Mountain News*: "Some Other Brand of Wealth," "Black Creek Sighting"; *Tendril*: "The Grand Piano Range," "Twisp, Washington " (reprint), "Crying Wolf," "Going Places"; *Black Mountain II Review*: "Her Big Scene" (reprint); *Telescope*: "Foreign Living"; *Apalachee Quarterly*: "Some Other Brand of Wealth" (reprint); *Ironwood*: "Chinese Mines" (reprint); *Spindrift*: "Finding the Tolt," "Literacy" (reprint); *Yarrow*: "Totems"; *Crab Creek Review*: "Washington Pass"; *Whale Anthology*: "Totems" (reprint); *Caprice*: "Morning at Lake Dorothy," "Squatter's Rights," "Begin the Beguine,"; *Pudding*: "Twisp, Washington" (reprint), "Literacy" (reprint); Metro Bus Poems: "If the Rain Never Stops"; *Pontoon*: "Totems" (reprint); *Iron Country*: "The Stairs at Franklin,""The Back Roads of the 50s" (reprint); *Willow Springs*: "Learning the Road"; *Matrix:* "The Back Roads of the 50s"; *International Poetry Review*: "Intersection"; *Pig Iron*: "Shine and a Hair Cut"; *Snippets*: "The Ticket Woman"; *Xanadu*: "Backcountry Collision"; *Devil's Millhopper*: "The Light at Sheringham"; *Spectrum*: "Cutting Cane"; *Arnazella*: "Don't Cry for Me, Argentina"; *Backbone*: "Peace Habits"; *Making Peace with the Bear*: "Peace Habits" (reprint); *New Delta Review*: "Ahtanum Ridge"; *Dalmo'ma*: "Healing"; *Contact II*: "Don't Cry for Me, Argentina" (reprint); *80 on the 80's*: "Literacy" (reprint); *Americas Review*: "Healing" (reprint); *Yomimono*: "Blue Herons"; *StringTown*: "They're All the Same to Me" (reprinted as broadside for Whatcom Poetry Series).

This project was supported, in part, by an award from 4Culture.

SBN 13: 978-1-936364-17-6
ISBN 10: 1-936364-17-4

CULTURE

Black Heron Press
Post Office Box 13396
Mill Creek, Washington 98082
www.blackheronpress.com

CONTENTS

LEARNING THE ROAD

LEARNING THE ROAD

In a town this small, they know a stranger
by the car they can't place. Know it
before they see your face inside,
a blank with no past, not Hank's wife
or the kid they taught in fifth grade—
the one that went bad years ago
and jumped town.

This week I sleep here
under a slim blanket in a rented room.
Mornings, the air is a white cold, rising
where the still pale fields breathe frost.

I want to learn this road.
I want to knock on these doors
with smoke fattening from the chimneys,
coffee on the stove, and people
moving half-dressed, shreds of sleep
around their skin like fog.

Black cows stumble slowly down the low hills,
dazed with cold. A horse leans
against the rail fence, the gate
where I could stop, turn up the drive
past dogs and the face coming sudden
to the window.

Something pulls me on, more hesitant
than roads, the curves I'll learn blind
just before I leave.
My name sits on my tongue like salt.

TWISP, WASHINGTON

Back east, they'd call these foothills mountains,
but you learn to map a different scale here
where the road west of you keeps rising
into a pass closed Thanksgiving to April,
where yards of rusted Ford bodies
and wringer washers aren't lack of pride
but history to people that don't read books,
a comfort of real things to talk
and tinker about, drawing off the restlessness
that comes between Saturday nights.

You could live a good winter here,
rent rooms in any grey weathered house
and watch the snow shift on porch chairs
left out ready for spring. Eat venison
and brown gravy at the Branding Iron
every Sunday, and walk it off
on the ridge behind the old copper mine
with that pack of scavenger horses and mules
snorting at your heels, and your own breath clouds
frozen at your lips like cartoon speech.
You won't need much talk here
where the names of things get crystal
and definite as that frozen air, something to exchange
hand to mittened hand on the morning bridge.
"Neighbor" is the guy who takes your shift
the day the baby's born. "Love"'s the years
of Saturday nights she's held your head above the john.

When the sawmill shuts down, the quiet
goes sharp and ebony behind a fine mesh of stars.
The creek runs louder than the road then, a sound
drawing you out to walk until the frost patterns your eyes,
and the cold burns in your blood like a hunger
for coffee and wood smoke, turning you back to town.

In one good winter, you could get so solitary here
that you'd forget the name for lonely,
until the spring came, surprised you
like the sound of ice breaking under the bridge.
It would be the day you swept the snow from porch chairs,
the night you stayed past closing in the Branding Iron
while the waitress shared Wild Turkey on the house,
let you talk until she turned the empty bottle over,
smiling, handing you the news the pass was open,
like a word she'd dusted off that morning
and knew you'd just turned foreign enough to use.

SQUATTER'S RIGHTS

For a century the hollow folk have lived almost without contact
with law or government. But soon the strong arm of the federal
government will fall upon them, for the land upon which they are
"squatting" is included in the area of a projected national park.
　　—Mandel Sherman and Thomas R. Henry, *Hollow Folk*

It turned out squatter's rights meant nothing,
like government meant nothing to the mountain folk
who saw ghosts walk these hollows every night
and never saw a flag, until the year
it called the place a park, skinned them
off these hills, clean as a squirrel pelt
lifted from the fat.

There was no fat here. Only a dust you scratched
to keep the skin around your bones
and chewed tobacco mostly, watched the blue haze
string itself each day between the ridges,
thick and slow as smoke from green wood,
smoldering up the Shenandoah Valley.

No name for the valley in this bastardized Elizabethan talk,
each hollow called simply after the first man that squatted in it,
splitting a few logs to live under. When you were born here
into some filthy rags the midwife wrapped, you stayed
and when you died, anybody fool enough to walk the hollows
heard the night wind kick up leaves, and swore it was your hant.
Every hant was mean. That was a fact, sure as your teeth
would turn black stumps before you got to thirty,
sure as a woman would count kids dropped

until she'd "had her number," and anybody
cutting fingernails on Friday would go insane.

That was enough to know. You never took the road
that passed eight miles from here
and you didn't need the flag riding up it
on the dusty hoods of federal cars, sudden
as the blight that hit the chestnuts
and left the ridge half-dead for years.

It turns out death is harder in the valley.
Every name gets written down there
and some stranger has to cross you off.
Only the moon stays friendly,
lighting your ghost up the steep
switchback road to the hollows, where a flag
won't walk at night, knowing a squatter
has no rights, knowing every hant is mean.

FIRST AVENUE

First Avenue, the heart of the city
where the blood comes in soiled
to be pumped back clean again
to uptown and suburb,
but the heart stays thick and dirty,
vicious with energy and the old noise
of dreams you hear in pawn shop windows
under their night lattice of metal and the lock.

You imagine notes like rusty glamour
rising from the pawned sax, pocket watches
swung on gold chains in a city of fat bills
swapped in back rooms, a grade B movie city
of dark Fords with machine gun windows,
ecru brocade ties and the ruby plush lips
of Hedy Lamarr.

The tagged Mix Master in the window
shuts your movie down. Obscenely domestic,
it turns the diamond to a Woolworth's, the sax
to bent notes the kid's got to hold
until the luck turns.

That's real then, like the vomit
and the curled-up drunks.
You feel like you want to wipe your shoes
and your hands pressed against the shop's glass.
But you don't. Because the real cleanliness is here
in the truths of First Avenue, where the blood comes in
stuffed with tickets you can't redeem.

THE TICKET WOMAN

Check her out the next time you go
by the porno arcade, the rhinestone flash
at her neck will put your eyes out
if the neon over her ticket cage hasn't.
You'll get the best look if you stand
in line, slip her your George Washingtons
she can stack with the other bills
that stink of cheap wine and stick together
with snot and the sperm wrung out
by celluloid lust. The cage window
frames her for you like a portrait,
all teased curls and black velvet bust, but not
voluptuous, just indifferent like her cat-green eyes
and the cardboard ticket she hands you
carefully, without touching. It's a distance
she pays good money for each week, her left hand
soaking in the sudsy bowl, her right in mine
while I scrub the nails, watch the week's take
of withered souls flake off her fingers.
She's the flesh and blood they dream of,
jerking off in their dark rows, imagining her
in every posture but the one I know her in,
serene as Buddha, holding her own dreams
of sunny morning falling through starched white curtains
to the breakfast table, to the man's face
she hasn't met yet, but carries
carefully in her manicured
and lotus-scented hands.

SHINE AND A HAIRCUT

for Nick

My father specialized in flat-tops
for years,
a cardboard sign in the barber shop window
curling in the Cleveland sun,
curls of hair my father swept into the dustpan
like a disinterested Don Juan, a man
afraid of keepsake lockets, what they hold.
My father was not sentimental.
An Italian
in an Irish neighborhood,
shaving cops and old men
while I shined their shoes.

A man likes to have his shoes shined
when his hair is cut, likes
to see the clean line of his ear mirrored in polished leather,
the white nape of his neck above the tan—
the last thing a barber does,
running the clippers there
before he flicks away the towel
releasing a stubbled cloud.

Faces shining out of shoes with pointed toes,
the kind of shoes Italians wear,
and Irish,
the kind of shoes my father wore, but not
the men in *Argosy* magazines
I read between shines.

Women hate it
when a man has his hair cut,
they don't love him
for days, thinking
how ugly logic is, how
hygienic
the burr from electric clippers
against their fingers
slipping behind his neck.
They keep their fingers there,
but let their eyes wander
to men on safari without razors,
unkempt as sensuality,
men in *Argosy* with dust on their shoes.

A man has to have a gimmick,
he thinks,
and to be Italian among Irish
is not one.
But what about a colorblind son with cakes of black, brown
and neutral in his kit,
a kid with smooth skin and dark Italian eyes
too innocent for a spit-shine in a New York subway
but this was Cleveland,
slow lines, time
to read *Argosy*, to think
about women, what shoes to wear for them,
what lines to give them.
My father lying to my mother
as long as he could
about his age, about his money,
gimmicks as flimsy as a cardboard sign.

What things women trying to love
forgive
and keep their fingers gentle on necks,
the careful generosity of lions
in a circus of spit-shined shoes.
A woman's world of cats on green-shingled roofs,
sleeping in their fur like jungles,
storing their passions in a locket
deep in their throats.
My mother brings the thermos of coffee
and all the curls lift from the shop floor
in the mute roar of her wind.

I picture women's foraging eyes,
flipping the streets like pages,
and the colors of them I can't distinguish,
only the gimmick of neutral, camouflaging their shine.
Forgiving the lines men give them,
lines that shift in and out of fashion,
but are always
like stripes on a barber pole—
peppermint,
ordered as logic
and the same.

TALKING WITH MY HANDS

You say my blood must be Italian, handcuff me
and I'd go mute. But I'm not Italian,
inherit no smooth olive-skinned language.
My wrists sprout Midwestern practicalities,
hands like my mother's, the red
raw floor-scrubbing talk
she draws shyly under the table,
while my hands break cover,
ride buses to the public library
where they study Houdini, all the ways
to slip the locks.

My hands caution me with old songs,
croon "take me as I am or let me go."
They paddle clumsily as happy mallards across your skin.
Each day I check for swans, hoping to metamorphose
in white gossamer eloquence along your thighs.

These words surprise my mother
who does not speak of thighs
except to say they are heavy.
On her finger the one set of rings she's worn
all my life, the small dime-store diamond
beside its honest band.
My father, coming to wealth now with some obscure
sense of apology and renewal, like any self-made man,
buys her new wedding jewels she wears
only in company, keeps in a blue velvet case
where they stay shiny as the family's sense of touch,
all the years we didn't pick the lock of love.

Now we meet and part in airports, awkwardly
trying caresses like artificial limbs.

These are the Midwest fields that speak,
apparent and dry as August corn, behind the patterns
of Venetian streets my hands weave. I make
disguises of motion, dazzle your eyes with gestures,
my fingers rippling like painted paper fans.

We are so wary, love feels
like a foreign tongue to us
in any language.
Pressed against your eyes, blind
as bats sounding the dark hollows of your face,
each fingertip wants to talk to you,
tell you how palmistry is a future we can slip the knot of,
like pasts we carry in the pages of old letters
and change each day, folding the words
through different creases.

Memory is a kind of hand-me-down
we translate carefully, skin stitched within skin
like an intricate fiction. My mother wrapping up her hands
for my birthday present, tying the ribbon with apology
for what I must inherit and reclaim.

Knowing such graces are plain, my hands
refuse to fold themselves in corners
or tug finger by finger into crocheted gloves.
They sit on my bed, haughty as old Scheherazades
wrinkled with cross-hatchings of plot,
demanding I make a truce with them, as Houdini

did with fact, the chains engaged so deeply in his tales
they set his hands free to keep on listening.
Those same thousand and one magics we hand each other
freely now, knowing how much depends on dawns
of not quite finished stories.

VOTING AT THE ZOO

It's Tuesday afternoon, a cold
election day with everyone at the polls
shivering so violently they hold the pen wrong
and vote Republican, rush back to work
and haul desks closer to the furnace vent.
You and I are unemployed, can't afford heat
so we go to the zoo, watch the gorillas
in their new cage. It looks impressively
like our vision of their real home.
The trees and vines seem sturdy enough
for Tarzan, who is always implied
when we build Africa, and justifies
the glassed-in patio, where two females relax
at home in suburban L.A.
The males are less gracious. They scowl
in the backyard, banging bits of jungle apart,
husbands on any Saturday afternoon.

Anthropology explains none of this.
Only Tarzan connects us, his vine-to-vine swing
bringing Pocatello and deepest darkest jungle together
like opposing forefinger and thumb—
an arc of imagination we rely on
to slip the cage.

LETTER TO LISA FROM THE SILVER DOLLAR TAVERN

Lisa, that moon we saw rise big last week
has set inside this singer's throat. His heart
breaks to a halting beat the band holds steady
like careful drunks crossing a kitchen,
keeping the booze in each step hidden, to dupe the wife.

Around me, army Quonset walls curve in like ribs—
memory of some war that never got this far.
Tonight the war's outside, like every night.
Red lights flashing on the street, another migrant
picked up. Their hats can never pass for cowboy.
A cop can spot the sporty angle at a distance,
name it Mexican, three syllables for "wrong."

The door's a border. Get past the cop,
then stop being white. I let my face dissolve
like smoke inside this dark. You know the method
and the taste behind it for a language
warmer than our own. *Con todo mi corazon*,
love's a serious hold on this dance floor,
heartbeat to heart. When the circle dances clockwise,
all hearts mend, like shaved moons waxing fat.

Dream this place, you'll dream beer, diced cactus
and salt. Good dreams to pack inside small borders
ribbed with war. Outside, the frost paints streets
and walls white. To get home, dupe the cop.

Lisa, I dream the walls might fall tonight
from this much spinning at the center.
All the jukebox quarters in my pocket sing like moons.

AHTANUM RIDGE

Tall grass, seeded with shotgun shells.
Locals shoot the old stoves dumped here,
their white sides blasted till the holes meet
and leave no further target.

We didn't have to fight the road's steep ruts
to know these hills packed guns,
could have read that in the valley,
the dogs on long ropes, the trucks pulled up
behind the bar. The ridge called anyway,
its pale spring curve of grass, shining
above the fields where hawks drift on valley mist.

One dead Ford leans against the sun,
balanced on its stripped frame, the hood
dappled yellow and grey around the bullet holes
like circus camouflage, the wide grill bared
in a growl. We slip our heads inside
carefully as a lion tamer's trick
and laugh until the chromed teeth grin.

SOME OTHER BRAND OF WEALTH

Taylor Sears had the first gold teeth I saw.
He was the only black in town then
and janitor to Main Street.
I watched him after hours, sweeping up cigar butts
and the dirt—as rich as gold in Illinois—
that farmers tracked across my father's office.
I told him jokes to make him put my eyes out
with his smile, a blessing he could flash me.

Then we got the Buick, gassed up Sundays
at Duke's Grocery on the edge of town.
Duke put paper Chinese fortunes in my ice cream
but all I wanted were his teeth.
He laughed the same slow noonday sun
as Taylor, and lived more solitary,
never drank in Main Street taverns
though his color was right
and his mother tried thirty years
to find a wife for him, till she gave up
and bought a trailer park in Florida.

My mother only warns me not to smile at night,
not to tempt pliers-fingered muggers with my mouth.
I know porcelain would be safer, and more feminine.
But I remember Duke and Taylor,
imagine the three of us drunk between cornstalks
or behind parked Fords outside the fairgrounds.

There's always a gold August moon
panning up like us, unpolished and startling

as nuggets in a farmer's whiskey.
A kind of after-hours flash, a fortunate laughter,
solitary, on the edge of town.

DEEP LAKE

Cabins at Deep Lake shut down for winter.
One trailer sits unhitched in the park woods,
maybe a migrant family, or an old couple
cutting loose at last.

Buffleheads pattern the lake,
slow wind-shadows fall through pine.
One big red-crested bird grips bark,
knocks this quiet into chips.

Nothing will stop the hope
inside that beak's hard constant swing.
The dusk light gathers on his back,
on isolate homes pressed against the road
where trucks pull into gravel drives.
Women switch on lamps in kitchens,
pound the night's tough cut of beef.

BACKCOUNTRY COLLISION

It was the usual—
fog across the windshield
and roosted on the barbed-wire fence,
in the headlights yellow and malignant
as a hen's glare.

I knew the road, where to reach
under its damp surface for holds on curves,
night towns I believed in
only when my wheels shuddered
over unmarked sets of rail track.

The bull was sudden,
solid out of fog,
larger than its daylight picture
tethered beside the culvert.

Night molding itself to sinew
and the long, ghostly stride of haunch,
a crescent horn crossing the dark
and raked down sheer metal.

Other headlights picking up the steam
rising between torn fog
from the heaped belly.
People on the road,
how I couldn't explain the feel of it,
something more than two unmatched shapes
on blacktop, how the fog
stitched itself back like time.

BLUE HERONS

BLUE HERONS

Every word and every letter is studied
and put into its fit place: the terrific numbers
are reserved for the terrific parts—
the mild & gentle for the mild & gentle parts,
and the prosaic, for inferior parts,
all are necessary to each other.
                    —William Blake, *Jerusalem*

I hated that old Spaniard in the next-door apartment.
He rolled up in his army overcoat each night
and spit the stars out, hacked his cheap pint-a-day
and black cigars. I'd hear his wife
hum through the sound, as if lullaby
could soothe that chest,
drown the rasp of pain in her ears.

Midnights, I'd wake and think that dry hack
must be herons, remember when they nested
near our cabin. I thought a bird that grand
should trumpet. Instead, they taught me
love sounds raucous, even in the blue throat of grace.

So maybe the Spaniard sat majestically on his horse once,
handing his wife a rose, his cape folding around him
like wings. Maybe she took his arm like trust,
with that oblique certainty of herons,
leaning half-diagonal onto one reed-slender leg.

Afternoons, he'd pace the park, mapping it
to military corners. I'd pass his wife
on the stairs, resting beside the window

to lift first one, then the other
brown-stockinged leg, to keep the blood
flowing. She pressed her face to the glass
and the Spaniard stared up, searching
for her eyes, like a throw of dice he'd trust
to come up lucky.

We get necessary to each other. We nest
in shared beds, elbows and knees shifting
the way a dog turns three times
before its limbs fit securely in sleep.
The talk begins then, whisky thick
and still majestic as Jerusalem.
It's the best we have: the raw, raucous hack
of archangels, that steady humming against the dark.

MORNING AT LAKE DOROTHY

Waking, I watch the morning's shapes of fog
drift casually as garden party guests
between the pines, gathering downhill
thick enough to hide the lake.
Their white mist turns you dewy-eyed,
as out of focus as Lillian Gish in some old movie,
smiling, dipping your red bucket in the stream.
Last night, we listened while that water sang
thin and high as chimes or children's harmonies,
spring snow-melt feeding the tune.
Now the fog draws silence in the air,
definite as the silhouette you left beside me in pine needles,
marking the way you sleep with one arm horizontal
like a tightrope walker, or the heron's long grip on sky.

We need your balance, need silence
and snow-melt talk, come here every spring
to write ourselves in pine needles,
tracing a shape to wear home.

Water's boiling in the coffee pot,
spreading an easy rhythm of comfort,
and across the lake a tree suddenly falls,
a quick sound splintering the fog
that drifts together again slowly
and steadily as habit, your hand pouring coffee,
balancing the day.

IF THIS RAIN NEVER STOPS

The rain breeds circles on the lake
as if a thousand trout grazed the surface.
Slate patterns meet, and meet again
and spread. Grey weeks like this
we dream the rain will never stop,
imagine we'll sink thigh deep in mud,
our feet turning to roots, each bone
branching twisted and brown.
When the moss covers our skin,
the days will nest inside our hands.

That's a vision we can't afford to follow.
We have to keep our minds fixed
on the trail, glistening like oil,
any step a possible sprain, a pitch
into the valley. The clouds
won't hold us up.
They're falling too, pretending
it's the quick way down
to the road and dry clothes,
hot coffee in the Mountain View Cafe
where everything's real again,
cigarette butts in an ashtray,
Sunday papers spread
across the counter,
the waitress eating eggs and bacon,
standing up.

THE BACK ROADS OF THE 50'S

What do they say,
those back roads of Wisconsin,
Iowa and Illinois? Say
slow towns, and kids with fast cars.
Say tight-curved gravel
with one-lane bridges.
Old Fords and Chevys drag the Main Street,
cruise the Arctic Circle's neon lights.
Girls with bare midriffs stalk the Tastee Freeze.
The swish of Goodyear rubber pours like summer rain
on hot streets, purrs behind young hips.

What do they talk
in Oshkosh and Springfield?
Talk silly at seventeen
and wise. Ice cream swirled
on their sassy tongues
and nowhere to go all night
but the back roads banked by cows,
cats' eyes in the headlights,
and the streets of town
with sleepy scattered lamps,
safe as chocolate malts and fries.
No New York pace of hustlers
and terror in the parks. No parks,
only cornfields dark enough
to steal a kiss, and burn
like wheels hanging on the edge
of some hairpin corner.

What do they say
in the back roads of Wisconsin,
the corn rows of Iowa, Illinois?
Talk hot lips, swear
backseat I love you's. Kiss
and the whole town tells.

THE TOWN TAVERN IN FAIRBURY, ILLINOIS

hasn't changed. The hunched backs
of corn and soybean farmers
still making the only mountain range
between Appalachia and the Rockies,
the Hamm's beer sign lighting bald spots
like neon moons. There's still somebody's son
half-pitching off his red stool,
one hand gripping the torn plastic seat,
his feet as short of the floor as my brother's were
in 1950, when my uncles fed him whiskey
till he gagged beside the Main Street lamp,
my father cursing when they hauled the kid home.

Whiskey lets them all curse—
damn the weather, the Commies at John Deere
conspiring against tractors, the big boys
at the grain elevator in Gibson City
and the bigger ones in Chicago.
They think nothing fattens here
except the bar maid's ass.
They weigh it weekly on the scales of pinches.
Under her Revlon mask, I dream the face
that served my brother, not much more
than a kid herself then, and already motherly,
filling his shot glass half with water,
giving my uncles the same teasing frown she wears now
carved into her face like a scar.
She ought to march in the Memorial Day parade,
collect insurance from the V.A.

Maybe she does. She's clearly sergeant here
and I'm as foreign as a Viet Cong in silk pajamas.

Their wives at home, or dropped
at some church bazaar, the sergeant's
the only woman men want here.
My presence buries them in silence
like dirty jokes with forgotten punch lines.
They can't curse, can't slip their hands
inside my shirt with a ten-spot. They know
my uncles, they remember my brother
and my father next door at T.J. Lyons,
selling them overalls and tan dress pants,
shaking their hands.

I'm as welcome as a hip priest
introducing electric guitar hymns
on a hung-over Sunday. They pray
for me to stumble toward the street lamp,
their eyes riveted on the Hamm's sign
where the face of god keeps coming up for them
in sky blue waters.

HER BIG SCENE

Aunt Mary could wring the necks
of two hens at once. Balanced
on spread feet and bony knees,
she'd stand broadside to the sun,
moving only her arms—
a grotesque of the pose I saw heroines take
in old Lubitsch films, explaining why they don't love him
to Melvyn Douglas or Gary Cooper.
I don't know who Aunt Mary loved then,
but she was proud as Jeannette MacDonald
and more desperate. Too tall, too thin,
and too far from Chicago, with Hollywood
only a place you drove to town to watch.
A distance her arms more than traveled,
whipping white feathers out of focus
till the necks cracked,
hearts still pumping headless spins
that staggered out against the coop.

My grandfather cut clean rows on the block
but she refused the axe like a Melvyn Douglas kiss.
I said she chose right, though I wouldn't touch a hen,
hated their glazed eyes, the smell of singed pin feathers
when my mother cleaned them—something Aunt Mary
never did. And never ate chicken,
only spun them beside the rusty pump
and walked the dirt road home,
kicking stones into the culvert like rejected lovers,
her fan mail staggering dead
against her rural route address.

THE STAIRS AT FRANKLIN

I

They built the two taverns
by the riverbank in Franklin,
a coal town, hung against the mountain
above Green River: wall tents,
and a row of company wood-frames
for ten bucks monthly.
The train cut past on the rock's lip.

Up there, miners' wives wiped in the view
with soot-black rags.
Children coughed in the belched train steam
thicker than fog.
And the cascade of stairs still descends
flight on flight to the river.

Could a drunk climb that zigzag line,
dark ladder up the south face of the mountain?
A wood step grows slippery green
with moss in this country.
Where the weight hits, the center
ripens, swells and caves with rain.

II

Put your left hand on the rail
and take mine.
No moon tonight, candles in our windows
lost in river mist.
I can still hear the laughter break

low over the channel rock in Green River.
A warm sound, the whiskey runs
warm in our hands.
I keep so close our breath clouds mix
before the fog takes them,
caught up into one white flame
like our candles at cold glass panes.

Do you remember now
how you carried me up this wood flight?
There were stars
and the fall-drenched cedar stung my breath.

Tonight, we rest halfway, floating
as children seem in sleep.
Our bodies shadows on the fog
as if already our ghosts climbed these stairs,
feeling for where the plank's rotted out.
Miners' ghosts, wise as bats,
our hands on the spectral banister
as now we step sure on whiskey dreams,
steady our weight against each other.

TRUE STORIES

for Cynthia

Merle Oberon died today.
The New York Times printed an old picture
and lied about her age
the way her face always did.
A Tasmanian witch, the years
cauldroned to nothing by her curved eyes.
Across dark rows, we watched her flickering magic,
our own spells buried under pleated skirts
and bobby sox fact.

She taught us fact is always ugly,
weak-chinned like the man who tried
to pick us up each matinee.
We slipped through the back door
and raced up the alley, laughing.
We suffered with her under the touch of boys
as dull as Melvyn Douglas, proprietary arms
they threw across our shoulders,
dangling sweaty palms above our padded breasts.

Romance was our carnival,
serious as the pact between red-spangled lady
and knife thrower's blade. A sleight-of-hand truth we trusted
like the white armor of knights Merle Oberon married,
one after another, and watched the dreams rust each time
beyond all conjuring.

This is the truth of stories *The Times*
could never capture. Only that she's dead
and the two of us must still leap

trusting the trapeze grip to meet us.
We won't hang the net under love,
though we walk now in bones
spliced like a film's 24-second frames,
our skin an honest tale we've learned to stitch
like Merle Oberon across false years,
the falling disenchanted numbers.

BEGIN THE BEGUINE

You wear black tie, which you would never
dream of wearing, but look at home in,
serious and thin as a Russian intellectual.
I am all pale silk, like these women
sipping champagne at round linen tables.
I cross and re-cross my legs
for the sheer caress of it along my thighs.
The band plays "String of Pearls." We rise,
glide counterclockwise in the line of dance,
precisely, your foot always where mine
has just left the parquet.

Desire makes an ellipse of time—
worlds we weren't born into
coming back tonight, sudden
as the Lusitania rising, the moon white
and a sideman's fingers pressing romance
from an old song.

Somewhere there must be a war
we haven't entered yet. Somewhere
Atlanta must be burning, and the producer
has just met Vivien Leigh.

SACAJAWEA COULD HAVE TOLD US
for John

Astoria, Oregon, is a grey town.
The half-shot neon of this one motel
too weak to fight the steady mist
that wraps the place, thick
with the beefy-shouldered ghosts of fur traders.

It must have worn the same vague weather
when Sacajawea stood above these cliffs,
watching the sea fall west into the Orient.
By then, she knew even China could not seem strange.
In the long weeks from Missouri
she had learned to hold waves and waving prairie
easily in the same heart, loving neither blue nor green
but wind—her way to keep what stays familiar
and still range, not needing the clear line
the two white men drew each day,
charting their last footprint,
calling everything between it and the sea
frontier.

They say frontier was gone by 1890.
Already just this dream of loss, half-remembered
like a deer's shadow leaping beyond headlights.
We inherit the white man's longing—
that conflicting love of settlement and space.
In Astoria, it almost quits.
The west is ocean and the mist blurs longing.
Here, memories sputter like old neon
lighting a run of good hunting,
a few famous Saturday nights.

Frontier is something you forget in school
like you forget to notice weather
after years of rain.

Only the dog outside our window
hesitates between some scent
and the whistle home. As if like us
he knew this grey blunts nothing,
knew loving stays a town we enter
wary as mountain men, who light a fire before dusk,
eat quickly, and move on into the dark.

THE SHRINE TO SAINT THERESA

The first bishop of Alaska built it.
He smiles, big chinned, in the photo
some priest snapped, full of well-being
like a man just rising from a plate of beef,
innocent of the ecstasies of saints.

Theresa must have warmed him
simply as the sun against black robes,
shining on church socials.
He cranked the ice cream handle.
The crowd applauded.

I like Theresa. I like her young,
a barefoot kid too big for sleepy Avila.
Not much for ambitious girls to do but die
martyred, or marry princes.

I like saints better than religion,
that promise of gold harps you get
for doing time on earth. I like the earth.
I like this shrine because it's earthy,
empty of almost everything but this quiet.
The pines crowd thick against it.
Waves half-surround the muddy spit of land,
wash the last edgy feel of church away.

A casual driver would miss the place. The road
wants to pull you north, past the unmarked turn
that's off the map for tourists
or pilgrims who want a miracle or blood.

Pine needles drift up the aisle,
sea weather blowing in the kind of natural saints
the unregenerate crave, like me, and local kids
who wheel in after sunset with their headlights cut.
The girls lie down and let the dried pine
press their cheeks like stiff communion veils.
They ask Theresa if this is love.
Better to ask Theresa than the bishop.
Best not to ask at all, assume everything
and love surprise. Bishop, I hope you're listening
in your crypt beneath the saint's bare alabaster toes.
It's always like this when we build a place,
each stone the beginning of some unsuspected blessedness.

ANCHORAGE HORIZONS

Forget height when you come here.
Forget the half-ring of mountain at the town's back,
the black geyser of ravens fighting skyward
from the railroad gulch each afternoon.
They built this town flat, built low
not to hug the earth in fear, like men in high winds,
but easily, sprawling across its surface
like fat lovers on sand, the feather-bedded slide
of drunks on sidewalks slick as bourbon.

No reason to stack homes hip by thigh
where every highway sign points north
and horizon is the only history worth repeating,
another name for separate. Only the bars fill,
packed against that last seasonless cold.

Here, love's like height—
no word for it. The bus pulls out past warehouse grids
and airstrip, stopping at vacant crossroads.
People descend, disappear to clearings
hidden in some long acreage. The rest forget them,
keep going to Nome and Barrow, where only the ice
stops them, the horizon paralleling sky at last
and even the days level into noon and midnight.

TOTEMS

for Bob and Jane

The herring ran this morning. I counted a hundred sea lions
packing the slim cut that runs past Juneau, reaching north
to salt marsh. In the sun, with no wind, the cold was nothing.
I forgot I could have wintered south, followed the eagles
that gather along the Skagit and Nooksack
to feed on spawned-out chum and coho washed up on gravel bars.
One eagle had hung back here, a long black knife
ripping the channel. Each time it called,
a humpback whale broke water, like some old sympathy
was strung between them.

If I've learned anything this year,
I've learned that clans are blood we choose,
not something written in the accidental line of flesh
like brother, cousin. My own runs north
and the gods I carve have winter names
that shine like frost in dawn. I live easier here,
keeping the totem like a stacked deck,
loon, fin, and bear's tongue shifting in my skin.

The Indians draw the thunderbird upright,
flying, riding the whale it hugs between its claws.
All alliances are strange—some old cry the blood follows,
those loved fingers in our hair at night,
the grip of shoulders, and the sudden breaching wings.

CRYING WOLF

In the weekend cabin we've rented
we haul our chairs close to the fire,
listening to the wind, wrapping ourselves
in afghans someone's grandmother knitted
on nights like this one. It could be
the frontier. There could be wolves
in those hills, I say, knowing
you don't believe me.

Like a kid skipping stones across a calm lake
you want no more between us
than this continuity of circles,
pleasant and non-insistent, the light banter of friends
in separate chairs drawn together only against the cold draft
that threatens the kerosene lantern flame.
I know you give me what you can. I make it easy
for you, like a witch tossing desire in her cauldron
to draw it out transformed for you
from dangerous wolf to reassuring wool.

Wolves oppress me too, like the rose light on the madrone
at sunset, the intense singularity of each branch.
The whole tree is easier to take in, blurred as a wolf pack,
as your figure beside me in the chair. But your chest
under the white shirt buttoned always to the neck,
the hollows beneath your eyes, your hands'
small restlessness—things sudden as a lone wolf
against a moonstruck cliff.

Tonight, I won't wrap my words with gentle laughter,
a comfort I've kept up for you so long.
Like a kid crying wolf too often
I can speak truly now and know
you won't leave your chair to hold me,
won't notice when my tongue turns
awkward with the howl of loving, when I look
carefully into the fire to say the wolves
are very near.

FOREIGN LIVING

Riding that bicycle
was like living in a foreign film.
The tires were thick, designed
for just going somewhere
slowly down dirt country roads,
shadows in the fields too grey
for Hollywood.

I liked the look of eggs
and undyed cheese in the basket,
white and honest like a film's subtitled talk.
Printed, the words seemed more solid,
everything less essential
cut for space. She loved him
or she didn't.

A bike like that, you can leave
anywhere you stop, leaning
against the first fence or tree.
It doesn't vanish. Only the lovers
go off-screen. By noon
the sun's haze bleaches words
they spoke that morning. They forget.

That spring you rode behind me,
the slow road curving uphill,
small cliffs on the right
cutting straight to sea.
The camera tracked us, wide angle,

in a long shot, the good French kind
with no music, everybody just knowing
"they love each other." So clear
we didn't even have to smile.

BEYOND CONFESSIONS

for Michael

I guess we're old and kind enough to be trusted to watch your daughter
while your wife leaves town and doesn't watch us. I guess there's wisdom
in the giving up of passionate touch that we gave into readily for years,
scalding somebody, or ourselves. Then, I used to think there were too
many confessions.

And so few sins now. Only these stolen beats of salsa that even strangers
in a dance class practice hip to hip. Or this brush of our elbows in the
kitchen camaraderie of chefs sharing big knives and wine.

Let me slip my fingers briefly as a comb's teeth through this silver
that's become your black hair. That much will feed our present, cost the
world so little, there'll be nothing to confess.

GOING PLACES

*In the realm of the imagination serious artists must be like Hart
Crane's tramps in their cross-country freight cars: They know a
body under the wide rain.*

Mark Shorer

Tonight let's not just lie here
while the train seven doors down
roars by and shakes the mattress
with fake travel. Let's go west
on those rails, but not
respectably in a Pullman,
rising to white linen breakfasts,
to steam delicate as early morning fog
on our teapot's silver,
and the waiter's gold tooth smile
brilliant as dawn.
Let's pull on our felt slouch hats,
low and rakish over the eyes,
hunch in the square padded shoulders
of Goodwill overcoats and go
with holes in our pockets, honest
as the truth of shadows that stretch
and shrink across the light of scattered campfires,
the ploughed cornstalks we'll stack and burn
to make some sense of place in the night,
the coal beside the rails as grim and useless to us
as the scrubbed sober code of dirt-farm kids
gathering isolate lumps of black in flour sacks.

Tonight, let's not turn dull back
to back, curled like separate fists

on what we think are dreams. Let's slip
like hands through honest pockets,
let the engine toss us loose as coal
and lie bone-lean and hungry for each other
under rain our tongues stoke warm,
the taste of it like cheap whiskey on our skins.
Nothing to huddle against but talk
and the thought of our slow walk tomorrow
to where the train stops,
slows long enough to swing on
and stretch hand to hand, rail to rail,
shadows slung together across a wide body of hope,
under the iron-thundered rhythm of going places.

FINDING THE TOLT

Under the suspension bridge across the Tolt
the last salmon are dying. They hang straight
against the current. They hold their ground.
A few turn and leap the wrong way, confused now
at the end. It doesn't matter. Their skin
will bloat and mange, decompose in the next mile.
The wind carries the sharp acrid scent
of death shifting into rich silt
feeding the flood plain.

Red-tailed hawks settle in trees. Flickers
sail ahead of me, across the path.
The fall is overripe, and the woods
turn the same muted colors as these birds.

I didn't think I'd find this trail again
without you. I never watched the road signs
when you drove. I saw the birds first
but you could name them. The distinguishing marks,
the third ring around a neck, the beak's bent tip.

One kingfisher, rattling like a child's wooden pull-toy.
It lands across the river. I see the limp,
silver curve draped along its mouth, the fish
it slams against the branch, over and over.
I've seen a mallard twist and jerk its neck
like that, caught in wire mesh like a harness.

Crazy gestures. You'd deny that, explain
the logic. Ratio of the neck's pull

against the wire's strength. Fish bones
the bird can't swallow till they're broken.

The sun that never broke the overcast
gets dimmer. When I leave the river
the path inside the woods is lost.
My boots sink in moss and dead log.
I am small as a fawn, coming suddenly
into these thick, directionless stands
of birch and ash, and suddenly afraid.

Go back. Follow the river to the bridge.
Don't turn and turn here, confused,
until the heart splits with panic
like a thin branch.

Look, trust is a compass, like love.
You can't explain it. I make these crazy gestures.
I twist my head so much I see the birds first.
I find this trail again, like salmon, without looking.
You're gone. It doesn't matter.

BLACK CREEK SIGHTING

What we understand
is distant
and framed, comes
like a heron
sighted from where the road curves,
from where the car turns west
and we are gone.
The glance of it,
the one reed-thin leg
crooked like held breath.

Tracings of cloud, the white
broken edge of wave.
Sky grey flat on water,
a vertical of shore grass,
and the heron,
its angle of sudden fragile dignity
against the shore.

THE GRAND PIANO RANGE

THE GRAND PIANO RANGE

The mining camp was there, you say,
matching the circle on your map
to the blonde lichen-covered basin below us.
No way to reach it but to scale these surrounding rocks
that turn near the top to knee and fingernail holds.
Gold in the hills, gold on the face of them now
while the long Alaskan sunset moves horizontally
across the sky, and I follow you into the meadow,
our boots sinking and springing up in tundra sponge.
I believe your map, and I believe the old miner
in the bar last night, telling us the woman
who ran the saloon here had a grand piano
packed in. All the way up the peak
I've pictured the thing wrapped in army blankets
strapped on the backs of mules, with bearded men
in red plaid wool shirts and suspenders
cursing, shoving at mule haunches
to keep them going together, and up.
You laugh at me, say of course they packed it in
piece by piece, keys and mahogany legs
stashed around slabs of salt pork and beans,
the only practical way. But what's practical
about a grand piano at 6,000 feet?
You'll say the woman had a football build,
wore brown dime store cottons buttoned over a motherly bosom,
the sleeves rolled back to fat elbows above the keyboard.
Maybe she did. Maybe that covered her
like every trace of the camp is overgrown now,
but I know she saw green satin in the washstand mirror,
tossed her head when she played

to let the gold sparkle at her ears,
touched fingers to her throat, like smoothing a feathered boa.
A vision of herself she hauled intact
through who knows how many claw-holds of years
spent measuring cheap whisky, her chipped nails
scraping the same jokes from the counter
like gold powder and grime. And loved the men anyway,
leaned into their wool shoulders as I do now
to match my step with yours, pacing out
this old mapped design, listening under your patient laughter
for hers, impossible and insistent as that keyboard's ivories,
necessary as these gold impractical hills.

CHINESE MINES

It mattered little to them
that the days stayed grey from fall to spring,
shades their drab jackets and shawls were lost in,
like herons camouflaged against the river.
They worked underground,
stooping before dawn into the copper mine.
The fine mist that takes the place of air here
meant nothing but more beams to prop damp cavern walls,
softer earth beneath dull shovels.

Perhaps the old story was theirs first—
the tunnel straight through the core to China,
all other passage home sewed up in company scrip.
Below their names on brown strips of paper
the figures grew, vertical as poems on a scroll,
a dark accounting tacked on counters
where they bought the foreign taste of venison
salted so thick their tongues swelled
and stumbled on the words of their own quick language.
In this new world, the color names they learned
were metal, blue crystals of copper sulfate
carried down to the railway, the ore's gold sludge
banking up in a waist-deep pond behind the plant.
Against the hills, their tin roofs rusted
into patterns as muted as sage.

The rain may have been a blessing,
a sound to count on, familiar and simple as lullaby.
A rhythm their bones take with them now
on the slow decay through the core, toward home,

leaving only this emperor's face on coins I rub for luck
as they did, the dreams thickening between my fingers
into a gold pond. There are robes on its shore,
shifting blue as herons in wind; in the air
quick laughter glitters, gentle
and constant everywhere as rain.

CUTTING CANE
after a story in China Men *by Maxine Hong Kingston*

To the island, they brought Chinese
working their passage to San Francisco,
and let them rot here for years, cutting cane.
The white devils said no talking in the fields.
But one day the men ploughed a big hole,
lay down with their mouths at the edge of it,
yelling in secrets, messages home, nonsense and curses.
We are making a new custom, they said.
We are founding the ancestors of this place.
After that, nothing to do but sweat,
wait for green shoots to blossom into story.

Say it's that. Or say it's just the wind
in the cane fields at sunset. Either way
a language I can't understand.
The sad old music it plays in me
is enough, like afternoons
on the porch, watching August rain.

The sun's flickering now between cane blades.
When it sets here, the island goes black
quickly. I'd never find the highway back then,
the miles of cane networked with red dirt roads
that could lead anywhere but home. I'd drive
until the headlights picked up long-bed trucks
unloading men, flares lighting the ghost sweat
beaded on their necks, pants knotted under their ribs
with twine. The night would settle into lungs
drugged with sweet scent burning from the mill,
the white crack of steel on cane.

THE KING'S ROAD NORTH OF KONA, HAWAII

The sign says prisoners made this road
and serfs who stuck their hands in empty pockets
when the tax lord came, and had to spend the winter
chopping stone. It could have been worse.
It could have been an Irish winter, cold enough
to freeze a hand like mortar against the rock.
At least the constant rain was tropic.
And the stone only long-cooled lava, full of air.
It split easily, weighed so little
a man could dream of juggling boulders
and did dream it, every night in the shallow pits
hacked out behind a half-circle of rock.
The same useless shelters
the more fortunate waited in, for permission
to cross the border into the next king's land.
Waiting, they carved the crust, cut stick figures
and spirals into the stone sea. The sign says
these told history or religion, accounts of how many
came on this trip or homage to Pelee, volcano goddess.
I guess they carved the rock singing
to drown the dry scrape of lava bits
that sets a jaw on edge. I guess the prisoners
sang too. And the penniless. Only a different song.
The kind of song the 'i'iwi sang
just before some servant trapped it,
taking a few prized red feathers for the king's robe,
setting the bird free to grow another season.
The robes took longer than the road then, but the road
took long enough that travelers wore a footpath first
beside it. Spirits walk there still, not caring

how faint the imprint's grown, traveling
by the feel of lives beneath their feet.
Once horses stepped that surely on the road,
so riders slept and woke up where they meant to.

I like to think the signs tell tourist lies.
I'd rather say it happened overnight,
that some old woman sat with Pelee
on this stretch of rock and thought it heaven.
That they spit tobacco, carving poems,
and just before the sun cracked open the horizon,
they danced a path so hard across the stone
the king's scouts came back to Kona
and said they'd hung his name on some new road.

BUFFALO, WESTERN NEW YORK

Ask the oldest waterfront bum
when the locks last spilled fresh water
into Erie. He'll spit and curse you
for talking like a tourist, tell you honestly
that brown is water's natural color.
You can't dream back the city's gracious past.
It's dead as the lake, the last roar
of Niagara in honeymooners' blood.
Steel wrecking balls smack the city daily
like a hot cue shot on brick.

The bars keep standing. Mill shifts
booze home, their GM wheels chaining through snow.
They smoke a pack a day in self-defense,
the first one lit before the kids wake,
before the sun rises over Attica.

The daylight turns the past brown—
that elm-shaded scene of sherry on the porch
and ladies in white linen. The edges of it
curl like withered snapshots. Burn it.
Buy a slick car, the kind the mafia buy
with juke box quarters. For grace
they wear white shirts to Mass,
drive plush loads of Sunday women past the pier
where old men stand, catching the same fish
each week, tossing it back.

THE LIGHT AT SHERINGHAM

Sailors call this an unforgiving coast.
The land's last thrust is rock here, slate
shelving over slate toward open sea,
no fine sand beach to cushion a run aground.
There are stretches here so desolate
you could wreck and walk lonely for days,
the road from the south dead-ended at Port Renfrew,
only the lighthouses going on, up the Pacific Rim,
the path they call the life-saving trail.

The light that Eustace Arden kept at Sheringham
comes early on the list, before the road quits
and the town names turn native. All morning
I've pieced together scraps of news
in the town museum, dating Arden's lamp to 1912.
The local papers show the island's two royal bloods
still met here then: Chief George, first
of a long line to wear a white man's shirt,
and Lady Emily Walker, who crossed the bay for dances,
velvet and tiaras under her rain slicker,
training her gold lorgnette on crowds.

What passes a coast like this, passes slowly. The change
of blood and habit in an almost frontier town
making a kind of history a man of long patience
likes to read, like weather. Arden read it
more than thirty years. He pulled the town around him
like a blanket, rising in the quiet four times each night
to wind the pendulum, the weights that dropped slowly
down the shaft, to keep the lamp turning.

Any place you shipwreck here, the weather wins.
What passes a coast becomes no more
or less than a shadow lit safely off the rocks,
an image of strange habits, like that English lady
the townspeople named "the old ship." Blood is a roar
the light splits, the only history you hear
climbing the night between the fall of weights
down steady towers, and the dream of your wife's elbow
thrust across the white, waiting sleep.

DON'T CRY FOR ME, ARGENTINA
for Eva Peron

This grave might hold your bones
or those some general's henchmen dug from peasant hills,
afraid your own might walk and knock cold fists
against his door. It doesn't matter, Eva.
The flowers in tin vases still hymn Santa Evita,
and the thick-flamed candles swallow humid nights.

You were right to wear diamonds.
To strike the sun that blind, this gravestone
should be diamond too. Then the days
would not ring so flat against it
like a speech a nervous village girl
rehearses in an empty plaza.

You owned five hundred hats to shade this sun
and cursed the generals under it.
Cursing is easy. The sins repeat monotonously
on fingers, and you learn the words young,
scratching them in village dust.

But hats, Eva, are various as birds.
You understood that, like you knew
this was a government of crows, blackening trees,
their nests lined with shiny bits like stars
picked up on village roads.
Crows are uniform as sin, and sing no song
hard and sweet enough to bother to remember,
unlike the kind of song a peasant girl can sing
in Argentina, who has a taste for hats.

Eva, does it snow in Argentina? It's hard
to imagine your grave cold, winter under this south sun.
If these really were your bones, they'd melt it.
The snow pouring red as blood, and people
shouting miracle or death, shouting Eva
peasant saint or criminal.

When the poor finally cry, they weep so long
dry rivers run and stone grows green with moss.
Their sorrow crowded dark beside your dying candles,
even the ones who wept before and cursed you
every time the dream you sang went bad.
Evita, you were right to say don't cry.
A star dies and the news takes years to reach us,
walking some dark road home, we see the light arc out,
and wish.

GUAZAPA, EL SALVADOR

Tonight, beside the usual beans
wrapped in tortillas, there is meat.
It means the strongest men and women
must fight again tomorrow.

Blue heat hangs above the village,
small fields and then green space
making a hedge against the government rifles.
When the soldiers fire, their guns speak English
like the Americans that fund them.

Pack now. Only what your arms
and back can carry. Give the children
something to hold. Walk all night
barefoot so the only sound is breathing.

When you reach the thick brown river,
it is morning. There are boats
but only two, and small. It will take
all day for everyone to cross.
Be patient. Believe the ones you left behind
will hold their posts until the night falls.
Remember soldiers stop their fire then
like city workers at a job.

One sunrise, parrots beat green wings
across the light, and it is over
for this time. Start home then
to houses bombed and pigs with cut throats,
no rooster left to crow the morning.

Believe burned fields can seed again
and blossom out of season. Yellow corn
to soak and grind into tortillas.
Believe the oldest woman in the village.
She has made this walk twelve times.

LITERACY

In Nicaragua where a poet shot Somoza
the children work the fields and orchards
in the morning. Afternoons, they sit
in schools. When they hear the bombers
of the *Contras*, they learn to hold
their pencils between their teeth
to keep their mouths open
so the thin drums of their ears
cannot explode
like air against the shock of bombs.

This is literacy.
This is the first power of words
inside a yellow stub of wood.

In Nicaragua, committees for defense
give vaccinations, teach children
how to read and write,
distribute rice and toilet paper
that are rationed now
because the country's harbors
are thick with foreign mines.
These things are called defense
in Nicaragua, where this word
means more than standing watch with guns.

To read and write is easy.
To be literate is something more,
is learning first the word
for struggle, and the sounds

of change. These words are written
in the seeds of cabbage, growing thick
in green rows, in the wood of homes
rising back where bombs dropped,
in the hearts held open
so they would not shatter,
in Nicaragua, where a poet shot Somoza.

.

HEALING

for Marta Alicia Rivera, a teacher kidnapped by the
Salvadoran National Guard

Blue night. The moon's leaned
half-asleep all week,
until it's filled,
a white eye shining
in the bruised dark.

She can't see in this bare light.
Dirt walls throw it back, electric,
only the fists block it,
clenched shadows falling
hard as light on bone.
She will never get up
from this floor.

A rooster breaks the slow heat,
hoarse with dust. She has listened
to that song for years. It used
to tell her something was beginning.
Now she wants this thing to end.

Real light falling on the walls
is morning. Two men lift a bag of skin
and the broken pieces shift inside her
like the letters of her name. She screamed it
over and over when they took her,
like the mother of a lost child, calling

in the streets. Calling herself back,
calling so the streets would know
what name was lost.

They want to cut her tongue
but her cracked jaw slants too hard
and blocks the knife.
Even without a tongue she knows
her throat would crow the end
of night. The streets would listen.
Something would begin.

The rooster means the children
wake and eat and wait for her
outside the school.
The rooster means the men
have beaten her since dusk.
She will never get up from this floor.

Dust in her mouth is a road.
The hands that lift her up are home.
Her hair is blood.
They have to shave her head to wash it.

One day, the women fill their shawls
with rice and walk to market.
On their heads, they carry baskets
of green onions, the stems
trail down like braids.

They trade these things for money.
They trade this money for a black wig.

They tell her, wear this.
They tell her this will cover you
until you heal.

PEACE HABITS

I
The women walk from Washington to Texas,
following the railroad tracks
that haul the nuclear waste.

A train rolls past, the flatcars
packed with sealed drums, deadly seeds
to plant in the Rattlesnake Hills,
in the Horse Heaven Hills, in the ground
where water gathers into aquifer,
then stream and leaf, gathers
into salmon egg and doe's throat,
into fountains and a glass.

II
Even the words are ugly.
Name them: nuclear, contaminated,
half-life, hazardous,
rems, cancer, waste.
Now try mountain, lilies, spring.
Store these words till you can sing them.
Store all good words in dowry trunks
like lace and hand-embroidered linens.
Save only this one word: stop.
Repeat it till it happens.

III
No green is green enough to name this slim marsh grass,
curving in the wind, bending as easily as girls let go their grip
on ground and cartwheel. The birds are flocking north
and stop to feed here. A thousand plovers and sandpipers,

quick wings and bellies shifting the sky brown, then white.
There are loons in the bay, striped with spring.
There are women in the grass, sitting so low
only their heads rise from the green like blossoms. A soft
rain drifts. A fresh water spring runs underground
and two women, leaning with their backs against a log,
can hear it sing. They start to hum and the others join them.
The tide carries the sound. Wherever waters
touch the land, it hums. Women fish in it, wade in it, scrub it
into freshened clothes, carry it in clay jars on their heads.
The hum becomes a heart. The heart becomes a language.

IV
Talk like a shaman.
Say "she told me something"
and mean "she turned my mind around."

V
If you cut a reed
and breathe through open stem,
blow a conch shell
or split a blade of grass
against your lips,
the note is D-flat.
Everything on earth
is tuned like this
and can be gathered
into song, to sing
beside the tracks of trains,
to pour like snowmelt
into spring's pure hum
of rivers being born.

INTERSECTION

*It is not the way of a Jew to make his work like there was no
human being to suffer when it's done badly. A coat is not a piece
of cloth only. A tailor is connected to the one who wears it and
he should not forget it.*
        Shmuel in *Number Our Days* by Barbara Myerhoff

So we are not parallel lines,
or we are, but live at infinity
where they tell me these lines intersect.
Geometry has no part in it.
But the needle does, and the thread stretched double,
the tongue moistening a finger to twist a knot.
Commerce has the least part in it.
Perhaps he is thinking, this stitch
between me and chicken's feet.
Chicken's feet are free at the market,
yellow and knotted as an old tailor's hands.
Perhaps it is cold today, raining
so that the air in the shop, the wool cloth,
even the bright steel needle
feel damp, his knuckles
feel large as the ceiling bulb.
Perhaps he is thinking of Sarah
at home in the kitchen
and Asher at the university in America.
He makes this coat for an American,
a small, dark woman who visits here.
To study the paintings, she says.
But he knows it is to study the faces.
He thinks she is looking for something or someone.

He thinks of this woman as he sews.
This, too, has a part in it.
Small like a hummingbird she is, and quick as that,
but her eyes are far away.
How this turn of a cuff will fall against her wrist
when she lifts her glass of wine,
it will break a man's heart to see it.
How this collar will lie warm against her throat
on a day like today, in a cold French spring.
He wonders how many times she will cry in this coat,
whether she will laugh.
Her eyes are so far away.
But he knows she studies the faces.
If only his hands were not so cold today,
so rough and raw it hurts
to turn the seam against the silk lining.
He thinks of silkworms, spinning out of themselves,
and the delicate fingers of Chinese women.
He turns the seam straight and flat,
though it hurts, though it would be so easy
to do it less patiently, to go home early to Sarah in the kitchen.
This has the largest part in it.
If the seam were not perfect,
if the sleeve tore some night
in the damp Paris wind, or in America,
some night walking home in the snow.
He has chosen the finest wool, thick and tightly woven,
more than the woman could afford.
It is his gift to her.
Because she sits in his shop
talking in broken French about paintings.
Because he knows she studies the faces.

Because the wind is cold when you find nothing
and he would stitch a collar warm and high enough
to blind her eyes from pain.
A collar intersected like a heart.
Because geometry has no part in it.

THEY'RE ALL THE SAME TO ME

The Americans brought down
in the World Trade Center,
the Pentagon and Pennsylvania.

The illegal maids and waiters
working in New York's twin towers.
The 5,000 Iraqis dying each month
under U.S. sanctions.

The Rwandans floating face down
in the rivers. So many thousands dead
in less than 100 days.

The hands chopped off in Sierra Leone.
The disappeared in Guatemala.

No limb worth more than another,
no heart, no hearth, no dream.

WASHINGTON PASS

Inside that intimate quiet of snow falling
I pick up the trail. The sky
has shifted all morning. First clouds,
then sun burning the path clear.
In a month, hunger will turn these grey jays mean.
The snow will shut their games down like the mountain,
small towns east of the pass digging in behind dead road.

I've made this trip five autumns to Twisp,
loving the town's slight brittle name
and the road's long drop from high snow into valley,
fall leaves torched up against dry hills.
Each year I cut the drive home closer to the first storm,
wanting the excuse to stay, socked in to some grey house
with four cords of split alder sway-backing the wall
and the back porch freezer solid with beef. The dream
is only half romantic. I've lived in small towns long enough
to know the isolation turns them mean as jays.
Snowed in, the meanness doesn't matter.
Somebody, cuts your face up, drunk.
Tomorrow, you need him for a poker hand.

That's as close to harmony we get, like separate stones
that pitch down cliffs together, and have no word
for avalanche. Against this white thick sky,
the geese call south, snow scrambling the sound
until the cries come back directionless
like a pack of wild dogs scattered in the clouds.
Tin horn notes, a rhythm I can't name desolate or glad.

Sibyl James is the author of eleven books—poetry, fiction, and travel memoirs—including *In China with Harpo and Karl*, *The Adventures of Stout Mama*, *China Beats*, *The Last Woro Woro to Treichville: A West African Memoir*, and, most recently, *The Grand Piano Range*. She has taught at colleges in the United States, China, Mexico, and, as Fulbright professor, Tunisia and Cote d'Ivoire. As writer in residence, she has worked for the Washington State Arts Commission, the Seattle Arts Commission, and the Seattle School District. Her writing has received awards from Artist Trust and the Seattle, King County, and Washington State arts commissions.